T0062880

Serenity Within Us

Serenity Within Us

TRIBUTE TO THE POET'S

DAVE GANESH

PARTRIDGE

To order additional copies of this book, contact
Toll Free 800 101 2657 (Singapore)
Toll Free 1 800 81 7340 (Malaysia)
orders.singapore@partridgepublishing.com

www.partridgepublishing.com/singapore

1//Greatness of Today or any given day, begin's with your positive, serenade self and perhap's a great smile too....

(Ambivalent Value:Courage and Self-Belief)

2//(Blue Like Jazz):A Love, A Relaxation, A Life and A Living through Jazz Music, will makes you smile, relax and ease the day through without worries….

(Ambivalent Value:Trust and Love)

3//No matter where you are, truly cherish your loved one's, your (Love and Care) are everlasting for them....

(Ambivalent Value:Caring and Love)

4//(Sweet Melody) of your's, to listen, to believe and to be aspired, within these crossroad's of life….

(Ambivalent Value:Appreciation)

5//(A quote from a friend):The Blessing's and The Grace's, are miracle's rarely to be seen, however miracle's do happen, trust me, it does....

(Ambivalent Value:Believe in God and Miracles)

6//(A Taste of new Happiness), with an new Valentine, just maybe, give it a try and never give up....

(Ambivalent Value: Happiness)

7//The Impersonation of Beauty and Art, begin's through with colour's of each women, truly....

(Ambivalent Value:Love)

8//Beauty and Good Heart's are through the eye's of each individual's and beholder's. Perhap's as well, beauty is actually everywhere....

(Ambivalent Value:Appreciation and Love)

9//Perhap's think of all good and happy thought's, then you'll see, happiness may come certainly....

(Ambivalent Value:Happiness)

10//Light's on, and there appear's to be our Fear's, Tear's and Far Cry that we face through our Life, but perhap's we could change these hurdles by seeing on the other-side.Perhap's we should next seek courage through(Humanity) values and hope through(Peace) values and all these virtues can only begin from you, you can make this world a better place to live in, look not further into fear's, look toward's The Bright Side, look toward's The Future....

(Ambivalent Value:Trust and Courage)

11//Friend's in need, are true friend's for life, look around and perhap's you will see an (Afterglow), you will never know, maybe, just maybe Happiness is around the corner, as Wilkinson (says)....

(Ambivalent Value:Self-belief and Happiness)

12//An Life that seek's for a chance and hope, within these crossroad's of Time....

(Ambivalent Value:Self-belief and Hope)

13//Look around, seek around and perhap's you will see an (Euphorisian), you will never know, maybe, just maybe there is a place for us, a new place, that place, where you, me and happiness are around the corner, perhap's....

(Ambivalent Value:Hope and Salvation)

14// Where to begin, where to end, perhaps you decide, as that's life one's again....

(Ambivalent Value: Trust and Hope)

15//Perhap's Man who do not forgive women, for their little fault's, will never then, see and feel their great virtues and love, it's within the simplest thing's, through (Aurora), a tribute to Women and Peace....

(Ambivalent Value: Aspiration and Tolerance)

16//(Love Story) make your life a lasting memory....

(Ambivalent Value:Trust and Love)

17//Live Life through the wonders you create, perhaps....

(Ambivalent Value:Vision and Mission)

18//What if? the person that was meant and right for you, is just around the corner, what if? as Tom Hank's and Meg Ryan say's, perhaps life has it's own way, slowly and eventually....

(Ambivalent Value:Aspiration and Love)

19//Love and Life, into what you make it of, depend's on you, as the music's through your ear's....

(Ambivalent Value:Inspiration and Aspiration)

20//(An Pilgrimage passage to his mother):Perhaps the wind that slither's and dances through winter's sky, may bliss upon your very eyes Mother, as within you, true love truly begin's....

(Ambivalent Value:Love)

21///(Mother)Your Love, Your Smile, Your Comfort, is a true treasure to us all, let's cherish the day that come's by bringing true happiness for our Mother's, as our Life and Love begin's through them, Happy Mother's Day everyone....

(Ambivalent Value:Love)

22//To Love and Be Loved, find (True Love) within the right partner, then you'll see perhap's True Happiness is possible, reachable by all mean's....

(Ambivalent Value: Love and Happiness)

23//For your view's, main changes occur's through, vital existence of Peace and Humanity....

(Ambivalent Value:Unity)

24// True love can still actually exist, if both Man and Women decide to mutually understand each other, perhap's ....

(Ambivalent Value:Tolerance and Sacrifice)

25//Fading through and within resilience of Man, Women, Life and Time, eventually what remain's is mere Hope….

(Ambivalent Value:Hope)

26//Ever through, I wondered in these crossroad's, where was the most charming gal you could ever meet, there was one that came across, an exceptional one, her name was(Leen)....

(Ambivalent Value:Trust and Love)

27///(Time of your Life), through matter's of, Family, Father, Mother and perhap's a Good Wife, bring's you an Everlasting Happiness, as some might say....

(Ambivalent Value:Trust, Love and Unity)

28//Within this time, through our prayer's and with each of our prayer's, it will be an invisible tool which then wield's itself in this visible world.(Pray for Turkey),(Pray for Peace).....

(Ambivalent Value:Hope)

29//A Metaphor of Changes in your Life, could happen, if you have an brilliant idea and will power to do so, by all mean's….

(Ambivalent Value:Taking Chances)

30//An Everlasting Life, begins with An Everlasting Freedom of your choice, choose wisely, perhap's….

(Ambivalent Value:Hope and Right Choices)

31//Love yourself, Love your family, Love your wife and perhap's Love your country, then you will see, what a wonderful world this can be?perhap's....

(Ambivalent Value:Unity and Love)

32//Entirely you are the one, that is utmost, in creating and changing your destiny, remember you're the one....

(Ambivalent Value:Self-belief)

33//As the wind waves through my eyes and immerse me in the Shallow Sadness, what remain's were you my darling, my angel and my only hope in this world, truly....

(Ambivalent Value: Love)

34//Blue in the water, blue in the sky or just,(you) blew me away....

(Ambivalent Value: Love)

35//A Stranger in a realm of fantasy, that fantasy good or bad, is your fantasy, perhap's....

(Ambivalent Value:Vision and Mission)

36//Perhap's in today's world, word's do sometimes, matter ....

(Ambivalent Value:Courage and Determination)

37//(Indian Wedding Bliss) //Where 2 soul's, come together as one, where Life and Journey of great love & true admiration begin's, for sister (Vicky)//....

(Ambivalent Value: Love)

38//Betrayals and Hatefulness still persist everywhere, within your willpower, be strong and walk through the line....

(Ambivalent Value:Courage)

39// Yes, maybe or No man, you choose….

(Ambivalent Value:Right Choices)

40//Today's world, do women truly can love a man, or love is just mere illusion that wonder's through....

(Ambivalent Value:Love)

41//Perhap's the vantage point to change one's life begin's by changing one's own word's....

(Ambivalent Value:Trust and Love)

42//Rewind no, Repeat no, Restart yes,(that's Life once again)….

(Ambivalent Value:Self-Belief)

43//Cherish your loved one's, as always, no matter where you are....

(Ambivalent Value:Trust and Love)

44//Love and Life, into what you make it of, depend's on you, as this music through your ear's....

(Ambivalent Value:Self-belief and Love)

45//*"It say's a person needs just mere, three things to be truly happy in this world: freedom to love, freedom to do your heart desire, and freedom to hope for, within this crossroad's"….*

(Ambivalent Value:Hope)

46//Greatness of Today or any given day, begin's with your positive, serenade self and perhap's a great smile too....

(Ambivalent Value:Self-belief)

47//Great Music, to (All) Beautiful soul's and to Beautiful morning, where sunset shine's and truly arise....

(Ambivalent Value: Love)

48//Nature, Forest, Greenfield, perhap's where true Peace and Serenity are….

(Ambivalent Value:Salvation)

49//Do not listen to other's all the time, sometimes do what your heart desires, you never know, what you may achieve, something magical perhap's....

(Ambivalent Value:Trust and Aspiration)

50//What captivates me through this sorrow and sadness, is mere hope and you, truly….

(Ambivalent Value:Hope and Love)

51//Plenty of Joy, Plenty of Laughter, Plenty of Happiness and Plenty of Us, within this twilight, perhap's....

(Ambivalent Value:Love and Unity)

*52//Be Bold, Strong and Sexy, if it's you,
so why not?*

(Ambivalent Value:Self-Belief)

53//An posture of yourself with self courage and self confidence, bring's the best of you, perhap's never give up and never look down....

(Ambivalent Value:Self-Belief and Courage)

54//There's rainbow within our world (w), but the colours of life's and race's, comes together in a country call Malaysia(ours), Malaysia truly Asia, as we say….

(Ambivalent Value:Unity and Love)

55//A Greater Day, A Greater (you), it may start from today, you never know, trust me and with best wishes to you dear friend….

(Ambivalent Value:Appreciation)

56//(Maya), a name that serenades illusion and captivates your imagination with passion, a pure passion it is....

(Ambivalent Value:Love)

57//(Helen), a name that could create, a thousand smiles, within a mere moment….

(Ambivalent Value:Admiration)

58//Self-Respect and Self-Defense, are 2 vital thing's, you should believe and carry on with (Life), as it saves you, from any dangerous situation, believe me, believe yourself....

(Ambivalent Value:Self-Belief)

59//Adrenalin, Anxiety, err, you just need, somekind of rush at times....

(Ambivalent Value:Self-Belief)

60//Certainly will, your will power to do so....

(Ambivalent Value:Self-Belief)

61//Love your-self, Love your family and never fail to Love (God), as true love and peace comes from the divine, eventually....

(Ambivalent Value:Believe in God and Miracles)

62//A Yesterday's Failure, will be Tomorrow's Success Story....

(Ambivalent Value: Determination)

63//A day of triumph will be a day to reckon your actual success story....

(Ambivalent Value: Courage)

64//An new revelation begin's from a new thinking, that new thinking process will then immerse into, perhap's a new Utopia....

(Ambivalent Value: Vision and Mission)

65// There was once, a Malay beauty captures my heart through a sudden moment, I could not even go near her, as this strong shyness appears within me.

She was not just a Malay beauty, I felt, she was thee brighter than any diamond I ever saw, she was beauty and grace(Rita)….

(Ambivalent Value: Love and Admiration)

66//(The Ragas of a Lifetime)sensuous melody and angelic rhythm that could brighten your very soul by (Anoushka Shankar) and Patricia Kopatchinskaja, ragas and love, perhap's....

(Ambivalent Value: Love and Admiration)

67//The Balance within the middle way, is perhap's the key to (Life)….

(Ambivalent Value: Hope)

68//Crisis is norm to (Life), however how will you like to go out from it, depend's on how you control your very emotion's....

(Ambivalent Value: Tolerance)

69//Fear kill's you, if possible, get rid of it, through your courage and determination….

(Ambivalent Value: Courage and Determination)

70//Remember True Joy, actually comes from the deepest sorrows....

(Ambivalent Value: Hope)

71//Say to strive. Say to be focus. Say to be like no once else. Say to be yourself, Say to make a difference....

(Ambivalent Value: Self-Belief)

72//All of us here, are reaching for somekind of (Happiness), what are your's?search it and owned it ....

(Ambivalent Value: Self-Belief)

73//I may go through hurdles, suffering, hopelessness, but I do believe one day (My hope and Effort would not be mere dust)as my hope are through this very writing's, may this writing's open up your Life and give you a new and resound Inspiration,(U)....

(Ambivalent Value: Hope)

74//4 fundamental's of respectful (Life) begin's by this core ethic's:

-Respecting other's and elder's without seeing the, (Race) code....

-Integrity within yourself and in what you do,(Focus) code....

-Helping other's in need,(with what you have),(Lending hand)code....

-Humble and be ease within yourself,(Peace) code....

(You'll be a winner, certainly will)....

(Ambivalent Value: Hope and Integrity)

75//Hatred and Jealousy are there around, you can't runaway from it, Just stay calm, be strong and put your faith in (GOD), nevertheless....

(Ambivalent Value: Hope and Integrity)

76//The Very coolest and The Very stylish actor of them all, is perhap's none other, but the one and only(Chow Yun Fatt), in every film's, he bring's in a new legacy,(with admiration)....

(Ambivalent Value: Admiration)

76//(Sir Rajnikanth) A Persona, that bring's an immense charisma, dazzling style, acting style with power-struck performance, within any given film, through this Era,(There's only one:Badshah)….

(Ambivalent Value: Admiration)

77// With every tear drop's, with every effort, with every courage, with every shame you go through, with every failures, (I bet you), there's one time, this one time, you will eventually succeed, by all mean's,(U)....

(Ambivalent Value: Courage and Aspiration)

78//(Rain drop's), (Tear drop's), or perhap's (You drop), nah,(Begin Again)....

(Ambivalent Value: Hope and Self-Belief)

79//(Those Past Year's)\\Great 90's, again....

(Ambivalent Value: Hope)

80//Sheila Majid (Simply The Greatest Singer), //(Antara Anyir Dan Jakarta), as always it will be,(with admiration) perhap's….

(Ambivalent Value:Love and Admiration)

81//Women(where inspiration's, and notion's of true love begin's from you)// (Wanita(dimana sumber inspirasi, cinta dan ilham bermula, hingga ke akhirnya) pertemuan....

(Ambivalent Value: Admiration)

82//Entirely, this is the love I am sharing with you, (You and I), our (Lifestory will be the greatest Lovestory), perhap's in time....

(Ambivalent Value: Love)

83//Anticipation or Innovation, I trust on Innovation, how about you?….

(Ambivalent Value: Hope and Aspiration)

84//Stargazed time, if there's a possibility to mould time, perhap's then past or future, can be a parallel of one (Time), you never know, this requires the effort of 5 geniuses, who can come together, and create the so called dream team, where are you guy's, let's unite and co-create....

(Ambivalent Value: Hope) \\18//

85//(Time Management) is (Self-Management), perhap's, think about it....

(Ambivalent Value: Self-Belief)

86//Through the sensation of fire, ashes of the earth, arise certainty....

(Ambivalent Value: Hope)

87//Thinking too much is restless, perhap's take it easy and relax, then just think again….

(Ambivalent Value: Hope and Integrity)

88//(In Life)do not waste time ever to mourn the yesterday's misfortunes, bad deed's, bad mistakes, as today will be your day, remember for why you should throw the Good over the Bad....

(Ambivalent Value: Hope and Integrity)

89// Think better today, tomorrow and even the day after....

(Ambivalent Value: Vision and Mission)

90//You are nature's greatest miracle, never waste you or your (Life)….

(Ambivalent Value: Hope and Self-Belief)

91//Swiss love or French love, as it's a matter of 2 heart's becoming one, perhap's....

+(As When Cupid Unfold's....)
(Ambivalent Value: Hope and Love)

92//(A Road Ahead), A Road to a newer Utopia, as only time will tell....

(Ambivalent Value: Hope)

93//May Goodness, the very last word's, prevail over Evil, at any given time, by all mean's....

(Ambivalent Value: Hope)

94//Through this crossroad's of life, I do believe that even a blind man or deaf women, deserves a normal life, equal right's and a education, as they too are one of (US)....

(Ambivalent Value: Hope and Aspiration)

95//*There was once, a Oriental Lady that came for my rescue(a light of hope), when I was absolutely starving, without money, ill in hunger, pain, no one around. She came gave me a hope, a chance, a life through this crossroad's.She was Saw, my dearest friend Saw(SK), a true friend in need….*

(Ambivalent Value: Hope and Admiration)

96//A journey or a walk to remember, can be decide by you, only you my friend….

(Ambivalent Value: Hope and Self-Belief)

97//As thing's fall mercilessly, you may then know the (Truth)....

(Ambivalent Value: Honesty)

98//(Trust in God)fear not anything, move life with courage, with fire, with yourself, with a winner....

(Ambivalent Value: Courage)

99//(Emerald, Gold, Diamonds, The Mysterious Beauty)//As the (Sun Arise) through the dawn of thousand night, The Tale of Arabian Night's Emerged from ashes and to be told, they say//....

(Ambivalent Value: Aspiration)

*100//(Life is a crazy ride, it is just crazy),
I on the other-hand only want's peace and
freedom....*

(Ambivalent Value: Self-Belief)

101//(A Rose Ivy), take a piece of Rose, give it to your loved one, that single Rose perhap's, sum's up a true love, that will begin....

(Ambivalent Value: Love)

102//Blue, blue, blue....This shades of blue, just turn me around....

(Ambivalent Value: Admiration)

103//Put your trust on something, be patient, be patient, work toward's of it and eventually your success may follow(As seen through The Malaysian Paralympic champion's)//(Extraordinary they were)….

(Ambivalent Value: Aspiration and Courage)

104//An posture of yourself with courage and confidence, bring's the best of you, perhap's never give up and never ever look down....

(Ambivalent Value: Self-Belief and Courage)

105//(Just As Today)it seem's to be an mellow down day, tomorrow just, just might be better, sometimes you got to be relax and follow the flow of life….

(Ambivalent Value: Tolerance)

106//There will be a metaphor arises from the beneath, through ashes of the earth, a fiery fire who sees….

(Ambivalent Value: Courage)

107//Devotion we seek, love we feel, we can, we can co-exist (to be one and together)with true notion of love, afterall…..

(Ambivalent Value: Unity and Love)

-A thinking man, wondering in wonderless of Depression, what a life, as he feel's?....

-A Friend, A Friend in need, A Friend for a Lifetime, as you always be....

-Immense Beauty and Grace, as always belong's to Tabu, Tabu the(Beauty)....

-//Sarawak //-Where Best of Nature, Sunset and Colour's of (Blue Sky), come together afterall....

-No matter where you are, truly cherish your loved one's, your (Love and Care) are everlasting for them....

*-(Sweet Melody) of your's, to listen, to believe
and to be aspired, within these crossroad's*

-Perhap's Man who do not forgive women, for their little fault's, will never then, see and feel their great virtues and love, it's within the simplest thing's, through (Aurora), a tribute to Women and Peace....

-(To the Wonderful Person's around the world), may internal sunshine bliss upon you, as your the guiding light that bring forth a more beauty, authentic and improve way of life, toward's us the community, cheer's and best wishes to you guy's, by all mean's....

-"There will be today, there will be tomorrow" perhaps then to make a better tomorrow, you should live your life fullest and meaningful today, perhaps....

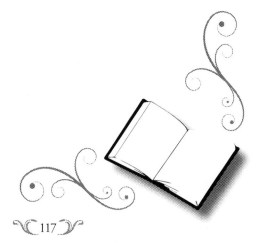

-Within you is a fountain of everlasting youth, it is through your mind, your talents, the sheer creativity you seem to bring to your life and the lives of other's. When you learn to tap this source, you by all mean's, will truly have defeated age and heart, at these crossroad's of Life....

-No matter what happen's in the past, let us not remain there anymore, forgive by all mean's and move on with better friendship, companion, as well a better life by trusting, helping and loving one another, by then Peace and Humanity will remain here truly....

-Nobody is sheer perfect through this world, however what remain's is your good deed's, thought's and value of contribution toward's of your family, friend's and community within your very own capacity, by all mean's then, you will see an Inner-peace, Happiness, Love and Joy after all, within these crossroad's....

-Through the Good Times or mere Bad Times, the journey of life still continues. Nevertheless have a faith within yourself and God, perhaps then thing's might not be narrow after all, only Good day's and Good times to be seen again....

-The Times of your Life, is only define through the path you choose to live, choose a good path and meaningful one, then you may see Happiness and Peace that come's from within, truly....

-Within great cinema, come's the greatest value. The Essence and Love of Cinema truly visualize and can be seen within (Cinema Paradiso), a tribute to Director Giuseppe Tornatore, thank you sir, by all mean's....

-Learn, Live, Love and Linger within your very own (Freedom)....

*-Perhap's music in itself, is an pure healing.
It's something we are all touched by and
remember, no matter what culture we're
from, everyone loves music through Heart,
Love, Joy and within Life Afterall....*

-A little thing's that you do or sacrifice for other's well being would not deter your life at all, as you can see them grow, have a better life within your virtues, why not help them, after all "Sacrifice is a part of life. It's supposed to be. It's a good deed and something to aspire to...._

-The pieces of your life will never come together, unless you have an vision, you believe in yourself and you believe in God, by all mean's thing's might change....

-Go make someone smile, laugh and even hug them if you may, you never know, within this slightest effort you do, you might bring joy to their life, let us make joy and happiness something reachable once again, by all mean's....

-At least once, for once in your lifetime, love someone sincerely, truly and honestly, as well help each other, by all mean's I guarantee you, your (Life Today) will be much more meaningful....

-Bitter Sweet Symphony of Life, you could change it, by putting trust on yourself And God, remember chase your dream's/ by all mean's, God will be there to help you and within you....

-Never be slave toward's 2 thing's, money and power, it will not bring you anywhere, look toward's of treating, enhancing and improving another person's life with what you have, by all mean's I guarantee you will win....

-Memories, what is life without the sheer memories of the past, those were the great time's....

-Take pride of being yourself, not just for today, tomorrow and year's to come, they say....

-Explore. Dream. Discover....live life with no regret's, no matter what other's say....

-Perhap's Life and The Journey Within are an (Endless Flight), you never know where you will reach next....

-This were and still will be a(Landmark Movie) in every level, Love, life, lesson and acquisition to change one's own journey is there, whether you literally take it or leave it there, by open.You decide.... (Amores Perros)as it is....

-Initiate an change toward's of yourself, by looking through and enhancing your self-esteem, this is where you need to begin and remember self-esteem build's up self-integrity, it's vital for one's own life....

-Remember, the only way we can learn is if we are exposed. And the only way that we can become exposed is if we throw ourselves out into the open. Do it. Throw yourself and be the change that you want to be in this world, cause this is your life and for once, own it....

-*"Imagine", Imagine for a better life within your term's, no matter what other's may say, because, this is your life, acquired as you only gona lived for once....*

-If you or I wanna make a change in this world, that's where we're gonna be able to do it. That's where we'll start. Every, Single, Time, by all mean's....

-Remember, "The things you do for yourself are gone when you are gone, but the things you do for others remain's as your legacy, through time....

-Perhap's it's enough for me, to talk about" Peace". I must believe in it. And it isn't enough to believe in it. I will work at it" by all mean's....

-Perhap's,.... Don't walk behind me; I may not lead. Don't walk in front of me; I may not follow. Just walk beside me and be my friend, that's all I need.

-Let us all play a part, to redefine's humanity and friendship that stay's within, afterall what are we without each other....

-Freedom within right's, why only women right's are upright all the time, Man also, do have sheer right's, why can't we create and initiate equal right's between Man and Women, we should learn to actually co-exist without limitation....

-Share compassion with other's and cultivate friendship no matter where you are, cause that's where (Humanity) relies on....

-*"The very first essential for success is a perpetually constant and regular employment of self-determination"….*

-The right to live, the right to be you and me, the right to have equal freedom, at the end of it all...

-A new (Hope) and (Dream), let us begin again....

-*"Life was never about finding yourself. Life is about creating yourself."* Go on and make a difference....

-Remember Life is not just to Live and Go, is actually to make a difference and be a betterman.Go on guy's, make a difference not by tomorrow or later, but at this very moment itself....

-Perhaps *"True friends are like diamonds – bright, beautiful, valuable, respectful and always in style." within this lifetime, God bless you Sahar....*

-A lady of your life, should be a mutual partner, able to uplift you further in life, enhanced you and lastly she represent's you, remember....

-*"Ambition and aspiration, they are both same things from different point of view, such in crazy and eccentric". Therefore, anything is possible....*

-*"Kindly within any given district or no matter where you are, look around you, there will be some unfortunate and disable people through the street's or corner, within your capacity, give food, shelter or a bit more, with what you have, at least for today, let's lift them up with a smile, by all mean's"....*

-(In Life), there will be a time, you will find out who you truly are and what you want, and then you realize that people you've known forever, actually don't see things the way you do anymore. So you keep the wonderful memories, but let go, let yourself move forward and feel free again....

-A solitude of night to be find, through the miseries of evening, perhap's....

-(Dualities and The Reminiscense Of True Love within a Lifetime), can only be seen and feel through within this Cinema, a real cinema on true love and aspiration in life.(Jason Scott Lee) true determination and versality of acting can be seen through here(Film:Map of the Human Heart)-(a talent to be reckon with, even today).On the other end, find a true, trustworthy, sincere and loving partner afterall, then you may see real Joy and Happiness within this crossroad's of Life and Time....

-Style and Substance, is a very essence of knowing who you are, being uniquely yourself and what you can create, within any given time....

-The Sweet Sunshine and Radiance of Smile from a women, only makes a man to look at her and see love, the very love that begin's....

-(The Radius of the will), is through your
determination and your true spirit from
within, nevertheless....

-"True Love" is not just about one's own desire, it's about feeling comfortable, safe, joy and happiness within your Best Friend, it's still there, never lose hope, look around, as it remain's to be seen....

-Live within matter, matter within Life, however true solace are within family, Love of a Family truly remain's....

-//I have fallen in love with English//and rest they say, were history….

-It's a practical world, that we live in today,
faced it, challenge it, but never fear of it....

-What if fine, wasn't good enough, what if, just if, you could have (Extraordinary In Life)....

Now:Your View's Matter's+

Printed in the United States
By Bookmasters